PORTRAIT OF
Singapore

PORTRAIT OF
Singapore

SEAN SHEEHAN

PRINCIPAL PHOTOGRAPHY BY RYNO REYNEKE

First published in 2004 by New Holland Publishers
London • Cape Town • Sydney • Auckland
www.newhollandpublishers.com

86 Edgware Road, London, W2 2EA, United Kingdom

80 McKenzie Street, Cape Town, 8001, South Africa

14 Aquatic Drive, Frenchs Forest, NSW 2086, Australia

218 Lake Road, Northcote, Auckland, New Zealand

ISBN 1 84330 598 4

Publishing Managers
Claudia dos Santos & Simon Pooley
Commissioning Editor **Alfred LeMaitre**
Publisher **Mariëlle Renssen**
Studio manager **Richard MacArthur**
Designer **Trinity Loubser-Fry**
Design Assistant **Jeannette Streicher**
Editor **Anna Tanneberger**
Editorial Assistant **Nicky Steenkamp**
Picture Researcher **Karla Kik**
Production **Myrna Collins**
Proofreader **Nicky Steenkamp**

Reproduction by Unifoto Pty Ltd
Printed and bound in Singapore by Tien Wah Press (Pte) Ltd

2 4 6 8 10 9 7 5 3 1

HALF TITLE PAGE *Thian Hock Keng is Singapore's oldest and most colourful
temple, built to honour Ma Cho Po, goddess of the sea and protector of sailors.*

TITLE PAGE *The gleaming, ever-changing Singapore skyline looks over one of
the busiest harbours in the world. A country with few resources, Singapore
has created this modern fast-paced city out of swamp and jungle.*

CONTENTS PAGE *This beautifully made up woman is performing in a Chinese
opera or* wayang, *an ancient mixture of song, dialogue and dance. She sings in
Cantonese or Hokkien and her opera troupe will perform all over the city in
marketplaces and cultural centres.*

THIS PAGE *Garlands of flowers decorate the shophouses of Little India. The worshippers at Sri Srinivasa Perumal Hindu temple buy these to leave as offerings
at statues dedicated to Vishnu the preserver.*

CONTENTS

INTRODUCTION

Early History

Singapura, Temasek, Pu Luo Chung – Singapore's earliest history emerges from ancient myth and sailors' tales. For thousands of years traders have been sailing around this peninsula and, perhaps even in the earliest times, using the island as a trading post. By the third century AD it had a name – Pu Luo Chung – meaning 'the island at the tip of the peninsula'. In the 13th century princes from the island of Sumatra ruled the island, now known as Temasek. For several centuries thereafter a settlement existed on the island, fought over by Siamese, Javanese and Melakan merchants who valued it as a trading post and a base for piracy, but by the 17th century the island was abandoned and used only by the Orang Laut (sea wanderers).

The modern name, Singapore, comes from a Malay story which tells of a prince driven ashore on the island in a storm. He saw a strange creature in the dense forest – probably a tiger – which he and his sailors presumed to be a lion, and so gave the island the name of Singapura (Lion City).

By the 18th century Europeans were fighting each other for a foothold on the Malay Peninsula in order to facilitate their lucrative Asian trade in spices and opium. The British set up a trading post in Penang in 1786, while Melaka was held by the Dutch. Looking for a better position, Stamford Raffles, an employee of the British East India Company, sailed up the Singapore River in 1819, signed an agreement with the local sultan and left 300 troops behind to stave off the Dutch. The colony of Singapore was born. Indian and Chinese migrants flooded to the island in search of work. As trade increased Singapore gradually became the administrative and economic heart of the British empire in southeast Asia.

By the turn of the 20th century a tiny British minority ruled over a largely Chinese population and by the 1920s Singapore was experiencing internal wars between rival Chinese clans as well as anti-colonial riots.

ABOVE *A 16th-century watercolour of the spice trade in the Moluccas (Maluku, Indonesia). The Portuguese were the first Europeans to arrive, in 1511. The English, French and Dutch came later, squabbling amongst themselves until the Dutch emerged as victors.*

RIGHT & ABOVE *A portrait of Stamford Raffles (1781–1826) and an illustration from his* The History of Java. *Forced to leave school at 14 and find work to support his mother and four sisters, Raffles educated himself and learnt several languages.*

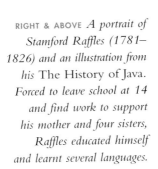

RIGHT *This 19th-century painting depicts fishing boats near Pasoeroean (modern Pasuruan), off the coast of Java, an erupting volcano providing an exotic touch. The Dutch first established a fort here in 1707.*

PREVIOUS PAGES *A statue of Sir Stamford Raffles, founder of Singapore, is framed by tall, sleek skyscrapers. The city has evolved into a modern hub of commerce in the region.*

ABOVE *The reversal of fortunes as the British formally accept surrender by the Japanese forces in Singapore in 1945, is depicted in this wax tableau at the Singapore Museum.*

LEFT *Fort Canning Park, built on elevated ground that provided a natural vantage point for Singapore rulers from the 14th century onwards. The British military had their headquarters here (now open to the public) before surrendering to the Japanese.*

The War Years

In December 1941 the Japanese forces invaded northern Malaya, moving rapidly southward on foot, bicycle and motorized vehicles, driving British-led troops before them. The objective was Singapore, but the British believed that the fortress island could never fall. Yet by February 1942, despite having little ammunition left and being heavily outnumbered, the Japanese received the surrender of the British in Singapore. Europeans were quickly rounded up and imprisoned at Changi Jail. Many thousands of Chinese men, considered a threat to Japanese security, were executed. Indians and Malays were allowed to co-operate but those who didn't faced execution too.

For three-and-a-half years conditions in Singapore grew grim as food was rationed, prices rose and daily executions interrupted people's lives. On 21 August 1945 the Japanese, losing the war and unable to maintain Singapore any longer, surrendered to the British. In the aftermath of war, military rule was established but by 1946 Singapore was once again a colony of the British empire.

By the 1950s it was obvious that Singapore's future lay in independence. Negotiations began and in 1959 elections were held for a semi-independent government. The new Assembly was dominated by a new party, the People's Action Party (PAP), led by Lee Kwan Yew. Lee became Singapore's first Prime Minister, a post he held for 31 years.

Lee's early years were marked by a struggle for complete independence from Britain. Opposition groups wanted to move much more quickly, but Lee saw that economic growth was the route to autonomy. In order to achieve this he sought a merger with Malaya. This would open Malaya's rich natural resources to Singapore markets and give Lee a valuable ally in his fight against left wing opponents.

In 1963 the Malayan Federation merged Malaya with Singapore and with the British colonies of Sabah and Sarawak. Matters went badly, though, and with the Malays quite fearful of Chinese domination, Singapore was forced out of the federation in 1965. In its stead, a fully independent republic of Singapore was established. The tiny island with virtually no natural resources achieved stunning economic growth, led continuously by Lee's PAP until the present day.

BELOW *Kranji Memorial and Cemetery, with names of the 24,346 men who perished in the Pacific War.*

13

Modern Singapore

From an island with absolutely no natural resources, little agricultural land, inadequate fresh water supplies and very little technology, Singapore has become one of the most technologically advanced and wealthy countries in southeast Asia. Its harbour is one of the busiest in the world, welcoming freight carriers and cruise ships alike, and is largely electronically controlled. Changi airport is one of the most busy and advanced in the world, while the national airline regularly garners praise and awards for its efficiency. In finance, communications, computer technology and banking, Singapore is a world leader and its population is both multilingual and well educated. Few homes are without computers, one in three people owns a mobile phone, and the facilities at some of the more luxurious apartment blocks are controlled remotely by their owners' cellphones. Traffic-flow and public transport are computer controlled while citizens can pay their taxes or contact their banks or order their groceries via the Internet or by phone.

Transport is also highly developed. The ultra-efficient MRT system (Mass Rapid Transport) moves people from the suburbs into the city while buses and taxis are controlled by global positioning satellites. Two causeways now link Singapore with Peninsular Malaysia and regular fast and efficient ferries ply between the island and its neighbours.

Singapore hasn't got where it is today without some sacrifices and a strict set of rules, and most Singaporeans will agree that the city-state has many regulations that can seem tiresome to strangers. A popular purchase among visitors is a T-shirt which lists all the banned activities in Singapore – such as eating on the MRT, jaywalking, importing chewing gum, setting off fireworks, smoking in public places – that carry heavy fines.

OPPOSITE *Icons of modernity, like a super-efficient airport and sleek skyscrapers, never seem out of place and are found everywhere. But authentic reminders of the past, like Anderson Bridge, built in 1910, tend to be concentrated in one small area of the city centre.*

BELOW LEFT & RIGHT *The MRT (Mass Rapid Transport) light railway system (left) reaches most parts of the island these days, while a cable car system (right) is dedicated to carrying passengers travelling to and from Sentosa Island.*

The Natural Environment

Singapore lies 137km (85 miles) north of the equator, extending 23km (14 miles) from north to south and 42km (26 miles) from east to west. Singapore's territory includes a number of smaller islands and its mainland continues to expand as land is reclaimed from the sea.

The highest point is Bukit Timah Hill at 165m (541ft). It is situated in the central granite hilly region which provides most of the island's water supply. The rest of the island is low lying and was once largely mangrove swamp and marsh.

Small areas of mangrove and rainforest survive on the island. In the northwest of the island, the Sungei Buloh Nature Reserve consists of 87ha (215 acres) of salt mangrove swamp which is home to more than 126 species of birds. Bukit Timah Hill and the MacRitchie, Peirce and Seletar reservoir parks comprise almost 3000ha (7413 acres) of parkland, secondary and primary rainforest, and an area of freshwater mangrove swamp.

Highly developed and land hungry, Singapore still supports a rich wildlife. Mammals to be seen in the reservoir parks include macaques and tree shrews, while monitor lizards are a common sight as well as chameleons and smaller lizards. Cobras, pythons, pit vipers and coral snakes also survive. Singapore's huge and diverse natural population of birds is added to by many migrants, as well as escapees from captivity such as cockatoos and the occasional hornbill.

Though animals can be quite hard to spot in Singapore, the plant life is abundant – from the exotic species growing in the Botanic Gardens to the strange mangrove trees with their aerial roots at Sungei Buloh and the elaborate orchids which spring from the trees along the island's many shady boulevards.

Singapore's marine environment is perhaps its most challenged. Heavy use of Singapore's waters by shipping has threatened much of the life of its coral reefs but conservation projects are under way to remove and relocate the surviving areas of coral. Several of Singapore's smaller islands still support healthy reef environments.

ABOVE *Despite being a highly technological and urbanized city, Singapore respects and protects its wildlife. You won't have to travel far across the city before you encounter beautiful blooms like this one.*

RIGHT *In Singapore the trees provide the city with much-needed shade from the searing heat. Trees grow everywhere, in the road verges, the parks and gardens and even straight out of the walls of the few remaining derelict buildings.*

LEFT *Long-tailed macaques* (macaca fascicularis) *are Singapore's most common primates. They occupy woodland areas such as Bukit Timah Nature Reserve and the parks around the central catchment area. Largely herbivorous, though they do not shun the occasional frog or crab, they occur in boisterous family groups of between 10–50 individuals.*

RIGHT *The brilliantly coloured white-throated kingfisher* (halcyon smyrnensis) *can easily be identified by its red beak and turquoise back. A resident though not very common bird of Singapore, it has a loud call and exists on a varied diet that includes not only fish and frogs, but small reptiles, insects and mammals.*

BELOW *The Malayan water monitor* (varanus salvator) *is one of the world's largest carnivorous lizards. It eats what it can swallow and is never found far from water.*

Ethnic Groups in Singapore

The Chinese make up 77% of Singapore's four million people, chiefly descended from immigrant workers hailing from southern and eastern China. They speak a variety of dialects, the most common one being Hokkien. Other ethnic Chinese groups are the Teochew, Cantonese, Hakka and Hainanese, each with their own dialect. In school, Chinese pupils learn Mandarin and English. Many speak a hybrid vernacular, consisting of a mixture of their mother tongue, English and Malay, known locally as Singlish.

Malays are Singapore's earliest settlers and make up about 14% of the population. They are descended from several other groups that once controlled Singapore. They largely practise Islam and speak Malay as their mother tongue, although like everyone else in Singapore they learn English in school. Women wear traditional clothes such as the *baju kurong*. Men are more westernized, but wear Malay dress for special occasions.

Indians make up 7% of Singapore's population. They originate from many different areas of the subcontinent

with the majority Tamil in origin. Singapore's other groups are the Eurasians, the descendants of marriages between Europeans and local people, and the Peranakan, the descendants of mixed marriages between Chinese immigrants of the 19th century and Malay women. These people developed a complex culture which was a mixture of the two races and has given rise in modern times to the wonderful style of cooking known by the same name. One million of Singapore's residents are foreigners, largely European workers on short-term contracts.

ABOVE *This old resident of Pulau Ubin, a small island off the east coast, still lives the traditional lifestyle of rural people. Today, most of Singapore's Chinese population is urbanized.*

RIGHT *Indians first came to Singapore in the middle of the 19th century as administrators, traders, teachers, engineers, and convicts. Serangoon Road is very Indian in style, but Indian people live throughout the island and inhabit all walks of life.*

BELOW *These Malay girls come from a community with a strong sense of identity. Once* kampongs *(villages) were the heart of Malay life; now Malays largely live in apartments, but this does not diminish their strong sense of culture or traditions.*

Festivals & Holidays

Singapore is an island for festivals. There are religious ones like Christmas, Hari Raya and Deepavali, as well as seriously secular ones like the great Singapore Sale or the Food Festival. The island also celebrates two New Years: the Western one and the Chinese New Year. Add to this the great parades of the Chingay Festival, the National Day Festival, the Hindu Fire Walking Festival and the compelling Thaipusam Festival when penitents pierce their bodies and walk the city streets, and just about every month is a good time to visit.

ABOVE *Thaipusam is a Hindu thanksgiving festival that is observed between January and February. It is characterized by dramatic scenes of devotees piercing their skin and tongue with metal skewers, hooks and spikes — apparently quite oblivious to the pain.*

LEFT *Brilliantly costumed, like some colourful exotic flower or bird, this participant of the Chingay Parade proudly displays her finery.*

RIGHT *No one burns real money in Singapore, but fake notes are generously roasted to a crisp during the Taoist Festival of the Hungry Ghosts as a way of appeasing any unhappy, earth-wandering ancestors.*

FOLLOWING PAGES *Chinatown, the area of Singapore that colonial administrators had demarkated for Chinese set-tlement, has lost much of its former character as a result of extensive renovation work. In the days leading up to the Chinese New Year, however, it regains its cultural dynamic in no uncertain terms.*

ABOVE *Christmas on Orchard Road is an explosive affair of colourful lights and flashing signs — an exuberant celebration in exotic style.*

LEFT *Orchard Road is also the main shopping hub for locals and visitors alike. Many bargains are to be had and superstores such as this one, offer every imaginable gadget and low-priced item, including a tempting free gift.*

RIGHT *The Dragon Dance is a custom that accompanies the Chinese New Year celebrations. Elaborate paper dragons are carried on poles that can be moved up and down to simulate the beasts' movements.*

BELOW *Drummers beat out a rhythm to motivate their teams in the Dragon Boat Festival in June. Once a local occasion, the event now attracts teams from around the world, most of them unaware that they are commemorating a Chinese patriot who drowned himself in 278BC as an act of protest against court corruption.*

Religions & Places of Worship

Singapore is officially a secular state, with the right to religious freedom written into the constitution. The most common religion is Buddhism, but many Buddhists also practise the other major Chinese belief, Taoism. About 14% of the population adhere to Christianity and about the same proportion subscribe to Islam. Hinduism, Sikhism, Jainism, Parsiism, Zoroastrianism and smaller sects also flourish on the island.

Several of Singapore's many fascinating places of worship – tiny, colourful Hindu temples, huge airy mosques, quaint 19th-century churches – have been designated national monuments and are among the oldest buildings on the island. Religious festivals play an important part in Singaporean life: from Ramadan, when Muslims fast from sunrise to sunset for a month, to the Hindu Deepavali, celebrating the triumph of good over evil, and the festival of the Hungry Ghosts when Taoists believe that their ancestors walk the streets.

OPPOSITE *The atmosphere of a Chinese temple is part practical, part mystical. Here, joss sticks burn in offering to the principal deity of the temple.*

BELOW *These papers contain the fortunes of people who visit the temple. The religious beliefs of the Chinese can range from ancestor worship to a belief in Buddha, or feng shui.*

ABOVE *Less than 15% of Singapore's population is Christian. The number of converts is growing, however, especially among the English-educated Chinese.*

LEFT *In a private moment, a Chinese Singaporean burns joss sticks at a small shrine and prays, perhaps for good fortune in some family matter.*

RIGHT *Sri Mariamman is the island's oldest temple. It was founded in 1843 by a Hindu who accompanied Sir Raffles on his second trip to Singapore.*

BELOW *The white skull caps of these Muslim worshippers signify a pilgrimage to Mecca. (Footwear must be removed before entering a mosque.)*

FOLLOWING PAGES *This colourful, elaborate gopuram, or entrance tower of a Hindu temple, is in striking contrast with the starkness of a nearby high-rise apartment block.*

The Arts & Entertainment

Since the early 1990s Singapore's arts scene has undergone a modest renaissance – with theatre, modern dance and music flourishing. The more traditional forms of art and entertainment have also benefited from a resurgence in interest. Theatre and poetry using Singlish and local dialects has flourished and, matching the new-found pride in Singaporean culture, have been the many government projects aimed at preserving and improving the island's architectural heritage. Add to this burgeoning cultural life the popular culture of food places, bars and bustling hawker centres and there is much to detain the visitor.

LEFT *The Singapore Opera regularly stages productions of international standard – operas, musicals and ballets. Here, a troupe of ballerinas drift across the stage in a scene from* Giselle.

RIGHT *Traditional Chinese opera, which seemed to be on the wane in past decades, has enjoyed a resurgence of interest. Today, theatre groups rediscover a part of their cultural roots that were once in danger of withering. Here, two ornately costumed participants act out a scene from* Tragedy of an Emperor, *a Chinese opera that is performed in English.*

ABOVE *The arts are alive and well in Singapore. Here a symphony orchestra performs in the Victoria Concert Hall.*

LEFT *A public statue of Salvadore Dali. Unthinkable a mere 10 years ago, it is emblematic of the government's willingness to embrace the arts.*

OPPOSITE *This quirky statue outside Sinagpore's National Museum seems to acknowledge the need for more than material satisfaction on the part of the island's new young generation of citizens.*

A Cornucopia of Tastes

For many visitors, Singapore's amazing range of festivals plays second fiddle to the diversity, quality and taste sensation of its food. Traditional Chinese cuisine flourishes alongside Singapore's own spicy Chinese cooking. Then there is a strange mix of Malay and Chinese cuisine called Peranakan, plus the lemon-grass-and-coconut Malay food. Throw in creamy north Indian sauces, south Indian vegetarian banana leaf dishes, hawker food, myriad European cuisines and the glories of Asian fusion cooking – well, eating in Singapore becomes a holiday in its own right.

Singaporeans love to eat out, especially seafood – whether at the local wetmarket surrounded by outlandish fruit and vegetables, air-conditioned food courts where banana-leaf curries share table space with Chinese vegetarian dishes and fast-food chicken meals, hip night-food locations such as Boat Quay, or in expensive western restaurants. In the food halls you will notice the halal stalls, where properly prepared Muslim food is sold, and see locals eating with chopsticks, knives and forks or just forks. Locally brewed and imported beers, exotic fresh juices and a variety of teas are always ready to hand from separate drink stalls.

BELOW *Once a notorious night spot where anything went, Bugis Street fell into disrepair in the 80s, but has recently been renovated and now offers stylish and inexpensive hawker food.*

ABOVE *No-one should leave Singapore without trying one of its national dishes. Satay is mouthwatering skewered and marinated pieces of meat. They are cooked over an open brazier in the street by the satay man and delivered sizzling to your plate with cucumber and satay sauce.*

RIGHT *The flesh of coconuts imported from Malaysia and Indonesia, yields a rich milk drink with the aid of a juicer. The fruit is more commonly used in Malay cooking, primarily for sauces and desserts.*

ABOVE LEFT *An old-fashioned food hawker prepares one of Singapore's traditional dishes. Singaporeans love to eat out in the evenings and inexpensive food like this is full of fresh ingredients.*

ABOVE RIGHT *Trays of steamed buns wrapped in pandanus leaves await delivery to the many hawker stalls that are located around the city.*

LEFT *In the wetmarket, stalls sell mountains of ikan bilis, tiny fish used to flavour Chinese and Malay dishes*

ABOVE *The exotic range of fruit found in a vegetable market varies according to the season. Expect to find rambutans, mangosteens, jackfruit, papaya, starfruit, coconuts, even the odd selection of apples or oranges looking decidely humble by comparison with tropical products.*

RIGHT *Alongside* ikan bilis, *this dry-goods stall also sells dried meats, potatoes and onions, garlic, Indian spices and many more exotic flavourings and condiments.*

AROUND
SINGAPORE

DOWNTOWN

The Colonial District

The elegant Raffles Hotel at 1 Beach Road is a renowned 19th-century institution that has been comprehensively renovated and is open to non-resident visitors. It has a small museum, which is open from 10:00 to 19:00. Nearby, across Bras Basah Road, is Raffles City, a beguiling modern cathedral devoted to retail shopping. Beside it is a real cathedral, St Andrew's, a gleaming white edifice that was built in 1862. While you are in the colonial district, look out for the Padang, the city-centre playing field, which is surrounded by some important colonial buildings. Opposite is a civilian war memorial situated in the War Memorial Park.

Also situated in the colonial district is the Marina South City Park, which was once nothing but wasteland, but has been reclaimed from the sea and is now dedicated to consumerism.

On the tiny hill above the colonial district is Fort Canning, an ancient historical site and now home to the Battle Box, an exhibition of the tunnels built under the hill and used by the Allies as their headquarters during World War II.

Raffles Landing Site, a quick walk from Raffles MRT station, marks the place where the entrepreneur first set foot on the island. Next to it is Singapore's new Parliament House and its predecessor, which is currently undergoing renovation to form an arts centre. Close by, on Boat Quay on the opposite bank of the Singapore River, is the Empress Place Museum, which is open on Tuesdays to Sundays from 09:00 to 18:00 and on Fridays from 09:00 to 21:00. It is home to a collection of artefacts from all over Asia and an object of beauty in itself. Beside it the Victoria Memorial Hall and Theatre is another Victorian edifice, still operating as a theatre. The bridge in front of the building is Cavenagh Bridge, erected in 1868 by convict labour.

PREVIOUS PAGES An enchanted evening view of the Theatre on the Bay, on Singapore's attractive Esplanade.

BELOW Raffles hotel was the site of Singapore's last tiger hunt and the birthplace of a famous cocktail. It became one of the most famous hotels in southeast Asia.

OPPOSITE Also on Beach Road is the War Memorial Park and a stark monument honouring all those who died during World War II.

LEFT *St Andrew's Cathedral, built in the 1850s using convict labour, once housed a bell donated in 1843 by Maria Revere Balestier, the daughter of Paul Revere. The bell is now in the National Museum.*

RIGHT *Parliament House is the oldest government building. It was built in the 1820s as a private home by George Coleman, the architect who designed much of early Singapore. The road beside it, High Street was Singapore's first road.*

BELOW *Cavenagh Bridge was constructed in Scotland's Glasgow in the 1860s. It was shipped out to Singapore where it was assembled using Indian convict labour and named after a now-forgotten high-ranking civil servant, Sir Orfeur Cavenagh.*

ABOVE *Empress Place was first completed in 1885 and served as the Immigration Department until the 1980s. It has benefited from two substantial renovations, a second one proving necessary when the foundations were discovered to be crumbling away.*

LEFT *Victoria Hall became the island's Town Hall when it was completed in 1862. By 1905 it had been transformed into a concert hall and today it remains an important venue for performances of classical music, ballet and opera.*

RIGHT *The Asian Civilisations Museum in Armenian Street, once the Tao Nan Secondary School, is an old colonial-style museum that tells the story of Singapore's Chinese heritage.*

ABOVE *Polluted in the days when it served as the island's main artery for the distribution of goods, Singapore River is nowadays only subject to the exhaust of bumboats taking visitors on tours.*

LEFT *There is little on the Singapore River to remind one of the days when it bustled with boat life. But it offers a fine vista for photographers seeking to capture the tranquility of water amidst urban architecture.*

The Waterfront

From Raffles' statue the waterfront is laid out before you. Boat Quay, once a collection of warehouses (*godowns*) and shophouses, has been fully restored and is now home to bars, cafés and trendy restaurants. On the opposite bank lies Clarke Quay, formerly also a crumbling area of deserted *godowns*, which now bursts with life and countless places to eat and drink.

RIGHT & FOLLOWING PAGES *The Boat and Clarke quays, riverside sites once characterized by busy waterborne trade, have been restored and are now popular areas of restaurants and bars where fairy lights create a festive night-time atmosphere and light breezes from the river make air conditioning unnecessary.*

The Esplanade & Merlion Park

The waterfront itself is now home to Singapore's latest beauty: the Esplanade, a $600-million 15-acre arts and culture centre with theatres, sculpted gardens, shops and restaurants. Following the coastline south, the waterfront boasts more well-established attractions such as the Merlion Park with its renovated merlion statue, and Clifford Pier, from where trips to the smaller islands and tours of the harbour set off. Here, too, is the Lau Pa Sat Festival Market, a renovated hawker centre and wetmarket. Built in 1894 in Glasgow and shipped out in pieces to be reassembled, it was known as Telok Ayer market for nearly 100 years. When construction work began on the MRT it was dismantled and put into storage, to be reborn in the 1980s as a tourist attraction.

LEFT *Lau Pa Sat really comes alive in the evenings when the city workers come out for dinner on their way home. The surrounding streets fill with tables and chairs and the delicious smell of a thousand different dishes. Street theatre groups entertain and craft stalls sell their wares.*

ABOVE *The ace in Singapore's rebranding of itself as an arts centre full of eastern promise is the bold Esplanade and its shells of steel and aluminium.*

RIGHT *The best way to see the city is from the sea, in one of the harbour's bumboats.*

LEFT *A large statue of the Merlion, the legendary half-fish and half-lion creature that was supposedly seen by 13th-century prince, Sang Nila Utama, when he first set foot on the island.*

River Valley

In the River Valley area, on Tank Road, is a collection of religious institutions, which illustrate the multicultural nature of the island. The Sri Thandayuthapani Temple, or Chettiar Temple as it is better known, is an important Hindu shrine. During the Thai Pusam Festival, penitents, their bodies pierced with metal spikes, arrive here after a processional walk across the city.

Close by is the Teochew Building, cultural centre for Chinese speakers in Singapore. A few doors along again is the Catholic Church of the Sacred Heart, one of Singapore's oldest Roman Catholic churches. In Oxley Rise stands the Cheesed El synagogue, while a little to the south is the Hong San See temple.

ABOVE *Situated west of Fort Canning Park, the colourful Sri Thandayuthapani Temple is most easily reached on foot via Clemenceau Avenue from Dhoby Ghaut MRT station.*

LEFT *Impressive and colourful, Sri Thandayuthapani Temple is a very distinctive landmark in the city.*

ABOVE *Hong San See Temple displays many architectural features common to classical Chinese temples. It includes the upturned roof with decorated ridge, as well as gilded panels and pillars carved with details of mythological figures.*

RIGHT *Hong San See Temple is a short journey by taxi from Sri Thandayuthapani, but an exhausting walk in the heat of the day.*

Orchard Road & Beyond

Every visitor spends some time in Orchard Road, browsing the countless shopping centres, enjoying the restaurants and night spots, and admiring the architecture. Some of the highlights are the imposing Ngee Ann City and the photogenic Tanglin Shopping Centre. If you can't find what you want somewhere in Orchard Road, it probably doesn't exist. It is hard to imagine that, 100 years ago, this glamorous and very urban area was a nutmeg plantation – hence the name – Orchard Road.

The Peranakan Museum is a showcase of the lifestyle of the Peranakan people, a mixture of Chinese and Malay. In the same area are Emerald Hill and Cuppage Road, where the 19th-century shophouses are preserved in their original style. To the north of Orchard Road stands the stately Goodwood Park Hotel, older than Orchard Road itself and still boasting its quaint 19th-century colonial architecture.

BELOW *The fortress-like Ngee Ann City shopping centre on Orchard Road features a multitude of shops, including a prestigious Japanese department store chain, as well as restaurants and one of the city's larger bookstores.*

ABOVE *Designed by the same architect who was responsible for the Raffles Hotel, the Goodwood Park Hotel has managed to retain a much more tangible sense of history and the colonial era.*

RIGHT *Lucky Plaza, a senior citizen in terms of Singapore's shopping centres, is very popular with tourists due to its high density of luggage and electronic stores; camera shops are another speciality.*

LEFT *Orchard Road at dawn, dominated by the pagoda-roofed Marriott Hotel at the junction with Scotts Road; below the hotel is the illustrious Tangs department store, founded in the 1930s and still one of the better places to shop in the city centre.*

ABOVE & LEFT *Built in a style known as Chinese baroque, the houses along Emerald Hill Road, just off Orchard Road, belonged to Peranakan families and were built during the first two decades of the 20th century. Among the first old buildings in Singapore to receive preservation status, they have now been renovated.*

RIGHT *The houses on Emerald Hill have been restored to their former glory and exude an air of contentment. Many have been turned into restaurants, inviting visitors to take a seat and admire the attractive surroundings while sipping on a refreshing drink.*

Little India

Singapore also retains the three ethnic quarters that were laid down during early colonial times. Serangoon Road is still clearly an Indian quarter with Indian-style department stores, a wet-market that specializes in Indian food, spice grinders, sari and jewellery shops and many redoubtable Indian cafés and restaurants serving the various cuisines of the subcontinent from fast-food vegetarian to specialist fish-head curry restaurants.

ABOVE *A common sight in and around Serangoon Road are Indians who transport their goods on bicycles that have been specially modified for this purpose.*

LEFT *Indian temples are often generously decorated with floral tributes, especially for religious occasions; small specialist stores like this one exist specifically to cater for such needs. Garland-makers busy stringing fresh flowers together can sometimes also be seen on the street.*

ABOVE *To the untrained eye, Indian stores along Serangoon Road seem to offer a highly eclectic range of merchandise, but much of what is on sale consists of goods and food-stuffs not readily available in modern-style supermarkets.*

RIGHT *This Indian food store retails fruit, vegetables and spices that are basic to Indian cuisine. Inside, there are sacks of strange-looking ingredients that are turned into different types of flour used to make* chapattis, naan *and* dosas.

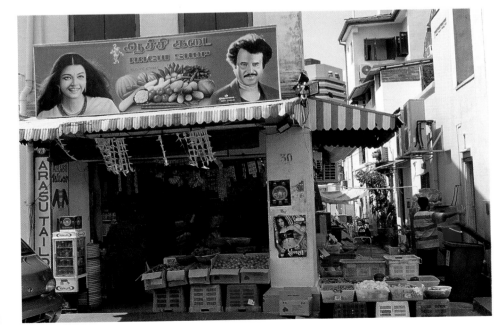

Arab Street

Arab Street, recently renovated, has Malay-style shophouses and is close to Kampong Glam (Sultan Gate) where the Malay royal family lived for generations. It is soon to be opened as a museum of Malay culture. Arab Street shops are gaily decorated with basketware, sarongs, pottery and a variety of items to pack into your luggage. While Malay-style restaurants are relatively uncommon here, there are coffee shops and informal north-Indian prata (savoury pancake) shops that serve tasty dishes.

ABOVE *Indian Muslim food is a speciality in Singapore. Worth tasting is* murtabak *(seen here being prepared), a leavened bread that is stuffed with meat and/or vegetables; when served plain instead, it is known as* pratha.

RIGHT *The Sultan Mosque on North Bridge Street, not far from Arab Street, was built on this site in the 1820s and is Singapore's largest. Radiant in the sunshine, its golden dome and minaret are enhanced by Arabic design features.*

OPPOSITE TOP *A run-down unreconstructed Malay-style house displays characteristic shutters and woodwork.*

OPPOSITE BOTTOM *The Malay shops on Arab Street spill their merchandise onto the pavement, protected by canopies and bamboo curtains.*

69

Chinatown

Chinatown is another distinctively ethnic area, renovated some years ago, but still with characteristic wetmarkets and Chinese-style stores selling antiques and curios, jade jewellery and much more. Chinatown is one of Singapore's oldest areas with some important temples and mosques. Although much of the area has been over-renovated and is now full of very exclusive shops and restaurants, there are still patches of the old life of this part of the city to be seen in the shops selling paper goods for funerals, as well as the Chinese medicine shops and the wetmarket in the Chinatown complex.

ABOVE *Old habits die hard: dried ingredients for Chinese cooking, not strictly necessary in an age of refrigerated goods, are available in Chinatown.*

LEFT *A view of the upstairs living quarters of elegantly restored Chinese shophouses in the heart of Chinatown; the shops below could have been anything from a tin-smith to an incense seller or a* popiah *(spring roll) skin maker.*

ABOVE *The upper floors of old-style shophouses display the characteristic high and narrow windows designed to provide maximum ventilation before the advent of air conditioning. From these windows would have hung washing poles and drying chickens, as well as the odd pot and pan too awkward to store inside.*

RIGHT *A small but essential green area for neighbours to meet and exchange news and gossip, outside a public housing block in Chinatown.*

RIGHT *Plants grow straight out of the wall in this unreconstructed part of Chinatown; mostly strangling figs, which, in their natural environment, would depend upon their host plants for support and nutrients, but have adapted to using cracks in concrete. The likely future of the ground the dilapidated yet atmospheric buildings occupy towers ominously in the background.*

SOUTH & WEST

Sentosa Island

The highlight of the south and west of the island is Sentosa, the 'island of peace and tranquillity', so named in 1972 when it became a leisure island. On Sentosa is Underwater World, an amazing piece of engineering which allows the visitor to walk underneath the habitat of marine creatures. It is open from 09:00 to 21:00 daily. Other places to visit are Fort Siloso, an excellent exhibition of wartime Singapore, the Butterfly Park, a pretty coralarium and, in the evening, the musical fountains. Destinations in themselves on the island are Fantasy Island, a swimming complex, and Volcanoland. Transport around the island is by monorail or cable car.

BELOW *Gardens, beaches and a plethora of eating places ensure Sentosa's popularity. Many visitors skip the theme-park attractions and head for one of the beaches – Siloso, Central or Tanjong – all with imported white sand and quite crowded, especially on weekends.*

ABOVE & RIGHT *Sentosa island's sandy beaches are looking their best for the daily visitors. Here one can stroll across the sands, or splash about in the water and have fun with inflatable cushions and the many other colourful paraphernalia of beach life.*

LEFT *The Musical Fountain's spectacular Dance of Fire and Water is a photogenic and harmonious celebration of fire, illuminative light, music and dancing jets of water. There are two shows every evening.*

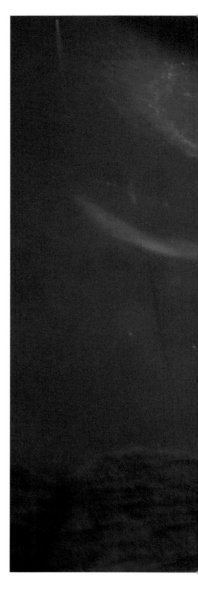

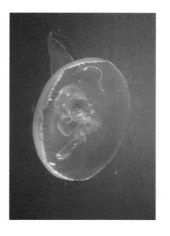

Underwater World offers one of the best experiences on Sentosa. A moving walkway (above & right) takes visitors below a huge tank filled with plants and sea creatures from some 350 species (opposite).

A special highlight is the scheduled appearance of divers floating through the water to hand feed some of the creatures of the deep.

ABOVE & LEFT *The Butterfly Park houses some 2,500 specimens – one of the largest collections of butterflies in the region. An environment replicating nature as closely as possible, it is a monument to the hundreds and thousands of these delicate creatures that have been lost due to increasing urbanization and deforestation worldwide.*

RIGHT *Sentosa, the largest of Singapore's offshore islands, is a pleasure resort girdled by a monorail. It offers a host of attractions such as Underwater World and Dolphin Lagoon, Images of Singapore, the Musical Fountain Show, the New Food Centre and a Maritime Museum.*

BELOW *This wartime scene recreated at Fort Siloso, recalls the days when Sentosa was the southern defence base for Singapore and its harbour. When the Japanese forces invaded in 1942, Sentosa's big guns were useless.*

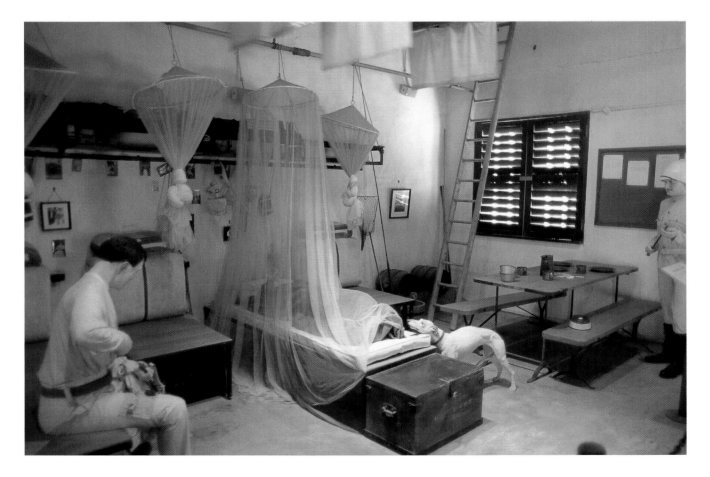

The World Trade Centre

The World Trade Centre is the chief starting point for a trip to Sentosa. However, it is a destination in its own right with lots of shops, the Guinness World of Records Exhibition, the Singapore Maritime Showcase and excellent places to eat. Adjoining it is the Singapore Cruise Centre where big ships on world cruises dock. Behind the centre is Mount Faber and the station of the newly refurbished cable car to Sentosa. Further north again is the elegant Alkaff Mansion (Telok Blangah Hill) once owned by a wealthy Arab family and now a sophisticated nightspot and restaurant.

BELOW *Though only 105m (345ft) high, Mount Faber affords fine views. It was named after the mid-19th-century army engineer who was responsible for building a road to the summit in order to facilitate a new signal station.*

ABOVE *The Singapore Cruise Centre, adjoining the World Trade Centre and a newly refurbished shopping mall are all part of a new harbour-front development that will have its own MRT station.*

RIGHT *What could be more enjoyable than riding high to Sentosa on a cable car from the recently upgraded Cable Car Tower? There is also the option of a boat ride to the island from the ground floor of the World Trade Centre.*

The Botanic Gardens and Haw Par Villa

Singapore's oldest national park, the 53ha (131-acre) Botanic Gardens in Cluny Road is open from 05:00 to 23:59. It is almost 150 years old and contains over 3000 species of trees and shrubs. There is an area of rainforest, an orchid garden, several lakes, concert venues, a café and restaurant, lots of birdlife and other small creatures.

Another wealthy family, the Aws, who made their fortune with Tiger Balm ointment, built the mansion on Pasir Panjang now known as Haw Par Villa. Statuary in the garden depict mythological themes and can be viewed from 09:00 to 19:00.

BELOW *Motivated by the hope of discovering viable cash crops, the Botanic Gardens once produced nutmeg, cotton, cloves and cinnamon. Although all of these ventures failed, the idea of an experimental garden never died completely.*

ABOVE & RIGHT *The tropical climate of Singapore supports some amazing plant life, best viewed in the Botanic Gardens. Roots, which in much of the world dig deep into the ground in search of nourishment, are aerial here — supporting a plant that can take nourishment from the atmosphere itself.*

RIGHT & FAR RIGHT *The National Orchid Garden in the Botanic Gardens houses some 700 species of orchids. Over 2000 hybrids have successfully been bred; the first, introduced by Agnes Joaquim in 1893, is now the island state's national flower.*

RIGHT *The entrance to Haw Par Villa suggests a classical Chinese garden governed by rules of symmetry. This cultural theme park with its interesting collection of off-the-wall tableaux depicts gory scenes from Chinese mythology.*

虎豹
別墅

New Ming village & The Science Centre

Travelling further west brings you to the New Ming Village at 32 Pandan Road. It is open from 09:00 to 17:30 when you can watch every stage in the manufacturing process of the typical blue and white Ming Dynasty pottery.

Further west in Jurong, at 15 Science Centre Road, is the Singapore Science Centre. Open from 10:00 to 18:00, Tuesday to Sunday, it is a great day out for children. Visitors can enjoy the many exhibitions, watch omnimax movies or spend a while in Snow City, a simulated arctic playground with a ski slope. Jurong also has two gardens on Yuan Ching Road, open from 06:00 to 19:00. The Chinese and Japanese gardens consist of themed gardens with their architecture and planting reflecting the various eras of Chinese and Japanese cultures.

BELOW *The Science Centre, benefiting from a recent multi-million dollar injection of cash, is awash with captivating displays, interactive activities and the wonders of technology. To get there, take the MRT to Jurong East and either walk the short distance, following the signs, or take a quick ride on bus number 335.*

ABOVE & RIGHT *Admission to New Ming Village is free. Here, visitors may well be tempted into purchasing a piece of the hand-painted porcelain that is on sale.*

LEFT *This bonsai graces a traditional Sung-Dynasty garden setting in the Chinese Garden. Each September–October, a display of lanterns lights up the Garden as part of Mid-Autumn Festival celebrations.*

OPPOSITE *The Chinese Garden is set on an island in Jurong Lake. A climb to the top of the stately pagoda offers wonderful views of the classically themed gardens set amidst the tranquil water of the lake.*

Jurong Bird & Reptile Park

The Jurong Bird Park located at 2 Jurong Hill, is open from 08:00 to 18:00 daily. This is a beautifully designed 20ha (50-acre) open park where 8000 or more birds happily coexist with one another. Beside the open aviaries there is a climate-controlled penguin house and a collection of night birds housed in a specially darkened environment.

Right next door is Jurong Reptile Park, open from 09:00 to 18:00, which is full of fearsome prehistoric looking creatures. Watch the crocodiles being fed or enjoy the thrilling stunts of the animal shows, which involve very dangerous creatures and real risk to the handlers.

BELOW Parrots aren't the only birds at the Jurong Bird Park. Visitors can also see multi-coloured toucans from South America. Occasionally, one flies off and surprises the residents of a Singaporean home by landing in their garden.

RIGHT *The Park offers various interesting shows, including Breakfast with the Birds between 09:00 and 11:00, and an exciting Kings of the Skies Show at 16:00. Children get to feed the smaller birds at any time.*

LEFT *Asian fairy-bluebirds* (Irena puella) *are easily identified by their brilliantly coloured backs and crowns. Inhabitants of lowland rainforests, they can be found throughout tropical Asia. They are fruit eaters, who are particularly partial to figs.*

LEFT *The blue-winged pitta* (Pitta moluccensis), *also called Little Forest Angel due to its spectacularly colourful plumage, is a shy little bird that feeds on a diet of small insects, snails and earthworms.*

ABOVE *A monorail glides visitors through the 20-ha (49-acre) Jurong Bird Park when the tropical heat proves too draining for a long walk. Either way you will see flamingos, kingfishers, woodpeckers and a variety of other exotic life forms.*

RIGHT *This iguana is one of the less fierce inhabitants of the Jurong Reptile Park, which also houses giant anacondas from South America and some alarmingly large crocodiles that reach 5m (16ft) in length.*

EAST COAST & CHANGI

The East Coast Park

Singapore's east coast is characterized by the East Coast Park, a long stretch of beach where Singaporeans go to swim, surf, cycle, and have barbecues. The park and the long expressway that lies behind it are part of a massive land reclamation project. Behind the expressway again is acre upon acre of housing, both public and exclusive apartment blocks with pools and fitness centres.

BELOW *Casuarinas, coconuts, screw pine and bougainvillea line the 16km (10 miles) of East Coast Parkway from Marina Bay to Changi.*

ABOVE *A deserted beach tells you this must be a weekday. Over weekends and in the evenings the beach is thronged with people doing tai chi in the early morning, barbecuing in the evening and jogging, sunning themselves and swimming in-between.*

RIGHT *A hawker centre on the east coast that offers fresh seafood, lots of chilled beer and a laid-back atmosphere. And all that just across the road from your high-rise apartment. Can life get any better than this?*

Malay Village

The east of the island is home to distinctive groups of people. Many Malays were moved to Geylang Serai when Arab Street was renovated and the area now has a distinctive non-Singaporean feel to it with older houses beside the rows of public housing blocks. The Malay Cultural Village is at 39 Geylang Serai, and open from 10:00 to 22:00. Traditional houses, crafts shops, a bird market, satay stalls and Malay-style restaurants attract Singaporeans every weekend who are nostalgic for the old *kampong* (village) life. Come here during Ramadan after sunset when the Geylang Serai market bustles with people breaking the fast of the day.

OPPOSITE TOP *The traditional shingled wooden roof of a Malay-style* rumah Melayu *house greets visitors to the Malay Cultural Village, where the crafts and traditions that are now less visible in modern estates are preserved.*

OPPOSITE BOTTOM *Quiet in the week, the Malay Village comes alive at weekends when Malay people from Geylang visit the restaurants and take their children to the cultural shows. For the visitor who wants to sample some of the culinary delights this is the best place to visit since Malay cuisine is rarely available in restaurants.*

RIGHT *Besides admiring the architecture and trying the food, visitors can also enjoy the high-tech shows that the Malay Village offers. Here you can see a traditional Malay wedding, watch the retelling of ancient Malay stories and wander through a 1950s-style* kampong.

Geylang & the Katong District

Katong, close to the Geylang area, has become a mini nightlife spot for local people. Along Joo Chiat Road are the traditional coffee shops where matchmakers once arranged marriages. There are also karaoke bars, some first-rate seafood restaurants and a decidedly non-touristy atmosphere. Unreconstructed Peranakan-style houses line the road, the lower storeys of which house the traditional shops of artisans who offer goods that have little place in a world of supermarkets and apartment living: springroll pastry makers and rattan furniture manufacturers.

The famous Crocadilarium, situated at 730 East Coast Parkway, is open from 09:00 to 17:00. The East Coast Park also has miniature golf courses, rides for children, sailboats for hire, fast-food places and many hawker stalls, especially at the East Coast Lagoon. The whole area comes alive at weekend nights.

BELOW The owner of Katong Antique House is an expert on Peranakan culture. At his shop you can buy your own little piece of the old Straits Chinese way of life to take home with you as a memento.

ABOVE *In the heart of Geylang Serai, which is a strongly Malay community, a Chinese temple flourishes. This is an indication of the tolerant multicultural society which Singapore has become.*

RIGHT *Joo Chiat Road and its surrounding streets are the best place to see beautifully restored Peranakan-style shophouses. These were wonderfully suited to their environment: long, high, shuttered windows offered cool breezes, and an inner open courtyard caught rainwater and fresh air.*

LEFT *Between the modern high-rise apartments of Geylang and the glittering amusement arcades of the East Coast Park, these shop-houses have survived – a tiny reminder of the old ways of Singapore, when life was slower and, perhaps, a little less complicated than today.*

Changi Prison and Changi Airport

The final destination on your journey east of the city is Changi, modestly attractive in its own non-touristy way with a village atmosphere, good seafood places and a pretty beach (if you don't mind the low-flying aircraft!). Changi Chapel and Museum is on Upper Changi Road North, and open from 09:30 to 16:00. It is a reconstruction of the chapel erected by the European inmates of Changi Jail during World War II. The museum has an interesting collection of wartime memorabilia, including some artwork and several secretly taken photographs, video footage and rare books. The Airforce Museum is also in Changi, at Block 78, Cranwell Road. Open from from 08:30 to 17:00, Tuesday to Sunday, it is a toys-for-the-boys kind of place, with exhibitions by the Singapore Air Force of planes and missiles.

Slightly to the northeast of Changi lies Pasir Ris, another specially constructed leisure area. It, too, offers a variety of tempting food courts, as well as the wacky Escape Theme Park with scary rides — and Downtown East, with more food courts and shops.

LEFT *A commemorative plaque reminds visitors to Changi of the many soldiers who lost their lives in the war.*

ABOVE *The little chapel is a replica of the one that was built by Allied prisoners in World War II. James Clavell's novel,* King Rat, *written in 1962, is based on their ordeal and survival tactics.*

RIGHT *The museum has a small but remarkable collection of artwork, mostly reproductions of the work of people who were once imprisoned here, but also photographs secretly taken by a 17-year-old soldier, George Aspinall.*

OPPOSITE & RIGHT *Visitors leave Singapore's Changi airport with an impression of immaculate, super-efficient organization. It is regularly voted one of the best anywhere in the world.*

BELOW *The attractive Expo MRT station, one stop short of Changi airport station at the end of the line, was designed by world-famous Norman Foster.*

NORTH OF THE CITY

Mandai Lake Gardens

The north of Singapore is perhaps its least developed area. At its heart are the green lungs of the island: MacRitchie, Seletar and Peirce reservoir parks. Most visitors who come here are interested in the really big tourist sights – Singapore Zoo, the Night Safari and Mandai Orchid Gardens, and these places are certainly well worth the bus ride.

Singapore Zoo, in Mandai Lake Gardens, is open from 08:30 to 18:00 and is reached by taking Bus 138 from Ang Mo Kio MRT station. It is home to more than 200 species of animals, has a dynamic captive breeding programme and allows most of its inmates a relatively natural environment. Close by is the Night Safari, open from 19:30 to 23:59, with nearly 50 recreated habitats. West of the zoo in Mandai Lake Road, and set on a pretty hillside, are the Mandai Orchid Gardens, open from 08:30 to 17:30. It is a working concern that exports orchids all around the world.

ABOVE & LEFT *A rewarding blend of the educational and the entertaining, Singapore Zoological Gardens is full of imaginatively created enclosures that bring visitors as close to its residents as is compatible with safety.*

ABOVE LEFT & RIGHT *Far less claustrophobic than most zoos, Singapore's calls itself, with a creditable degree of justification, an 'open' zoo. Animals are restrained by moats and wide ditches; cages are kept to a minimum. The inhabitants, such as this gibbon (left) and bearcat (right) obviously feel quite at home here.*

RIGHT *Quaint shuttle buses trundle visitors around the zoo. Popular night tours bring you astonishingly close to nocturnal animals.*

LEFT *Unlike most other members of the feline family, the Malaysian fishing cat (Felis viverrina) does not mind getting its paws wet as it inspects the pond for its next slippery meal.*

BOTTOM LEFT *The tapir, known locally as* badak tampong, machan, cipan, tenuk, badak murai *and* teronok, *is often mistaken for a fierce creature due to its odd size and shape. It is, however, a shy forest dweller and tends to avoid confrontation with man.*

BOTTOM RIGHT *The Malaysian tiger is under threat due to habitat loss and conflict with man. In order to protect it, the Department of Wildlife and National Parks of Peninsular Malaysia created several Tiger Management Units in 1976, the same year in which the big cat was officially declared a protected species.*

OPPOSITE *Bearcats, known locally as* binturongs, *are members of the palm civet family. They are arboreal mammals that relish fruit, though they will also eat carrion, fish, birds and eggs.*

Bukit Timah Nature Reserve

OPPOSITE *The northern part of Singapore is home to commercial orchid growers, the largest of which is Mandai Orchid Gardens. Many of the orchids on display here have been bred by the owners. The big gardens are open to the public and make a pleasant addition to a trip to the zoo. Some of the hundreds of types of orchid on display are for sale. If you see something you like they can arrange to have it packaged and shipped to you.*

RIGHT *Singapore is one of only two cities in the world to have a significant area of primary rainforest within its boundaries. The 81ha (200-acre) Bukit Timah Nature Reserve, only 12km (7.5 miles) from the city centre, contains more species of plants than the entire North American continent. At its heart lies Singapore's highest point, Bukit Timah Hill at 162.6m (533ft) above sea level. Well-marked paths lead through the jungle. Along the way, walkers can see exotic birds, butterflies, inquisitive monkeys, squirrels, flying lemurs and other wildlife. The reserve is open daily.*

At the southwestern edge of the green belt is Bukit Timah Nature Reserve. The exhibition hall at 177 Hindhede Road is open from 08:30 to 18:00. To get there take Bus 171 from Orchard Road. This interesting reserve comprises large tracts of secondary forest with a few patches of untouched virgin rainforest. Macaques and other wildlife roams the woods and there is an interpretive centre as well as forest trails to explore. This has to be one of the best days out that Singapore has to offer, and it's free!

Three Chinese Landmarks

There are three very Chinese sights in this part of the island. Kong Meng San Phor Kark See Temple is a huge temple complex, one of the largest in the region, with various pagodas and meditation halls, a turtle pond, and an old people's home. Situated on Bright Hill Drive, it is open from 06:30 to 21:00. Come here on Vesak Day in mid-May and help celebrate the Buddha's birthday. South of the temple, on Tai Gin Road, is the Sun Yat Sen Memorial Hall, open Tuesday to Sunday from 09:00 to 17:00. This is where the Chinese nationalist leader lived in the early part of the 20th century and where he planned the overthrow of the 267-year-old Manchu Quing Dynasty of China. At 184E Jalan Toa Payoh, in the middle of a public housing estate, is the Siong Lim Temple, open from 06:30 to 21:00. Over a hundred years old, it was recently renovated and now has a Dragon Light Pagoda topped with a golden spire.

ABOVE & RIGHT *Lian Shan Shuang Lin Shi, the official name of Siong Lim temple, translates as the Twin Groves of the Temple of the Lotus Mountains. It is a functioning monastery and inside the various buildings are ornately decorated panels and deities carved in wood and stone.*

OPPOSITE ABOVE & BELOW *The ornate exterior of the late Sun Yat Sen's villa and the reclining Buddha calmly reposing inside.*

LEFT *Kong Meng San Phor Kark Temple, not a regular stop on visitors' jaunts around the outskirts of the city, is surprisingly spacious and covers over seven hectares (17 acres) of land. A visit is especially worthwhile on Vesak Day in mid-May, when doves are set free to celebrate Buddha's birthday, death and attainment of the blissful state of nirvana.*

ADJACENT ISLANDS

Exploring beyond Singapore

Around the island of Singapore is a whole archipelago of tiny patches of land, all part of the Republic. Many of these are simply holding bays for oil refineries, firing ranges for the armed forces or even tiny coral reefs with no land at all, but several are green and accessible with good fishing and snorkelling opportunities.

South of the island you can hire a traditional motor bumboat from Clifford Pier and potter along to Sister's Islands, Pulau Hantu, Pulau Semaku and Pulau Renggit. These are all tiny patches of land, glittering in the southern seas, off the main tourist routes, with clear waters and coral reefs. Much more popular with locals, and accessible by regular ferryboat from the World Trade Centre, are the islands of St John and Kusu. Kusu has a Chinese temple and a Malay shrine, both very popular with local people. It can get crowded on certain days of the year when Taoists, particularly, flock to the temple. Legend says that two mariners, a Malay and a Chinese, were saved from drowning when a huge turtle picked them up on its back and transformed itself into an island. The grateful men duly built two shrines to honour the turtle. St John's is positively luxurious with toilets and changing rooms and decent beaches for swimming.

If it's an idea of pre-modern Singapore you're after then the best place to visit is Pulau Ubin. This is a little gem of rural life with sleepy kampong houses with chickens and goats running about, coconuts helpfully falling down from the trees, lots of tiny shops selling a few basic items and lots of winding roads to cycle and appreciate the calm. All this is only a mile or two from one of the most technologically advanced cities in the world. Secondary jungle covers much of the island. At the furthest side from the tiny harbour are seafood stalls to which people come from far and wide to eat. The island has two good beaches and even a tiny, spartan resort if you wish to stay there. Pulau Ubin is accessible from Changi Point Jetty. Creaking bumboats fill up with passengers and take off only when there are enough fares to pay for the trip. The ride there lasts only a few minutes, but is a little adventure in itself.

ABOVE *The first thing visitors see when they step ashore to Pulau Ubin is the village centre — some grocery stores, bike hire and cafés. The very few wooden buildings still remaining in Singapore are here. Life here is similar to that of a Singapore village 50 years or more ago.*

ABOVE *A Malay* kampong house, built up on stilts and surrounded by all of life's necessities. Chickens in the yard, coconut trees for shade and milk, as well as goats, fruit and veg, are all examples of what you would see.

RIGHT *Once a very common sight in the shallow waters around the island, quaint stilt houses built over the water, such as this one on Pulau Ubin, are now a rarity.*

RIGHT *This is Tua Pek Kong temple on Kusu island. It is dedicated to the Chinese god of the soil. Climbing up the hill behind this temple takes you to Kramat Kusu, a shrine which is dedicated to the Malay spirit Datok. Childless Malay couples come to the kramat to pray for children. Both these places of worship are very popular destinations for pilgrims during October and November.*

FURTHER AFIELD

Excursions

To the north of Singapore stretches Peninsular Malaysia, a fascinating mixture of rural *kampong* life, high-tech cities, idyllic coral islands set in crystal blue waters, and vast tracts of virgin forest. To the south are the Riau islands of Indonesia, with their own culture and beach resort attractions.

An afternoon trip over the causeway into Malaysia takes you to Johor Bahru, a noisy, busy place, utterly different from the ordered Singapore. Here you can eat at Malay coffee shops and check out gleaming new malls. At night seafood stalls and some brash nightclubs open.

A two- to three-day trip, will take you to Melaka, the ancient trading kingdom on Malaysia's west coast, with its pretty beaches, historical sights, craft markets and Peranakan and Portuguese heritage – ancient winding streets, a city *kampong*, antique shops which will have you wishing you had more room in your luggage, and the quiet, sleepy atmosphere of a town past its heyday.

An hour or two by train from Singapore brings you to Kuala Lumpur, the capital of Malaysia and a rapidly developing metropolis. Singaporeans travel here to shop, taking advantage of the lower prices. Here you can enjoy the best of luxury restaurants at reasonable prices, explore Chinatown with its chaotic streets, eat prata from a streetside stall or take a tour of the city's historic, colonial architecture. Museums, a beautiful craft market, high towers, peaceful mosques and, at the heart of the city, Merdeka Square where once the British played cricket.

From Singapore, a flight in a tiny aircraft takes you to the island of Tioman where accommodation ranges from simple to luxurious. There are miles of beaches, coral to snorkel around, watersports, a mountain walk across the island, boat trips and superb local food.

To the south of Singapore are many tiny Indonesian islands to explore. Batam is the most accessible, with regular ferry services from the World Trade Centre. A 40-minute journey brings you to Sekupang from where you can hop on to another boat to explore one of the less developed islands, or head off to your hotel to enjoy the beach life. Transport is by taxi and, while there are several small towns to visit, beaches and nightlife are the main attractions.

Bintan, largest of the islands in the Riau archipelago, is about three times the size of Singapore. Visitors mostly stay at one of the resorts on its northern shore, but the intrepid can explore stretches of untouched jungle and kampongs. This island offers much indigenous culture – from fishing villages on stilts to temples and night markets.

ABOVE *The 17-century architecture of Melaka, the city where the winds meet, stands as a testament to its former glory as a bustling entrepôt at the heart of the trade routes.*

ABOVE *Fishing the traditional way, this man's daily routine is a far cry from the international events hosted at the World Trade Centre, a mere 40-minute ferry ride away.*

RIGHT & FOLLOWING PAGES *If you leave on a morning flight from Singapore you'll be snorkelling, diving or sunbathing on Tioman island by lunchtime. Energetic visitors can hike the inland trail that cuts across this island, which lies off Malaysia's east coast.*

INDEX

Italicized entries indicate photographs.

PHOTOGRAPHIC CREDITS

Copyright rests with the following photographers and/or their agents. Key to locations: t = top; b = bottom; l = left; r = right; tr = top right; tl = top left. (No abbreviation is given for pages with a single image, or pages on which all photographs are by the same photographer.)

AFP	Agence France-Press
BAL	Bridgeman Art Library* (*see* footnote)
Ff	Ffotograff (CP = Carl Pendle)
GC	Gerald Cubitt
Gg	Gallo Images / gettyimages.com
HW	Hugh Webb
IP	Impact Photo

JG	Jill Gocher
PA	Photo Access
STB	Singapore Tourism Board
TC	Tom Cockrem
Ti	Travelink (GC = Geoffrey Clive; AE = Abbie Enock; CM = Colin Marshall)

front cover		IP	26	t	JG	65	t	Ff / CP
endpapers		Gg	27	t	PA	72–3		Gg
1		Gg	27	b	Ti / AE	76		JG
2–3		AFP	28		JG	76–7		JG
4–5		IP	29		JG	82		IP
6–7		JG	30	t	JG	86–7		JG
8–9		IP		b	Ti / CM	89		HW
10		BAL[1]*	31	t	Ti / CM	94		GC
11	tl	BAL[2]*		b	Gg	100		TC
	tr	BAL[3]*	32–3		JG	101		TC
	b	BAL[4]*	34		TC	102–3		TC
15		IP	35		TC	108	b	GC
16		TC	36	t	TC	109	tr	GC
18		GC	38		JG	110		GC
19		GC	39	t	JG	111		GC
20		TC	41	b	JG	113		STB
21	t	TC	44		TC	118		TC
	b	JG	52–3		Gg	119		TC
22	l	JG	54		JG	120–1		TI / GC
	r	IP	55	t	TC	122		TC
23		Gg	62–3		AFP	123		JG
24–5		Gg	64		Ff / CP	124–5		JG

*BAL[1]: Giraudon/Bridgeman Art Library. *The Spice Trade in the Moluccas* (1555), by Guillaume Le Testu (ca.1509–73).

*BAL[2]: The Stapleton Collection. *A Ronggeng Dancing Girl*, plate 21 from Vol. 1 of The History of Java (1817). Thomas Stamford Raffles (1782–1826).

*BAL[3]: UK/Bridgeman Art Library. Sir Thomas Stamford Raffles, by James Lonsdale (1777–1839).

*BAL[4]: UK/Bridgeman Art Library. *Volcano and fishing proas near Passoeroean*, by Thomas Baines (1820–75).

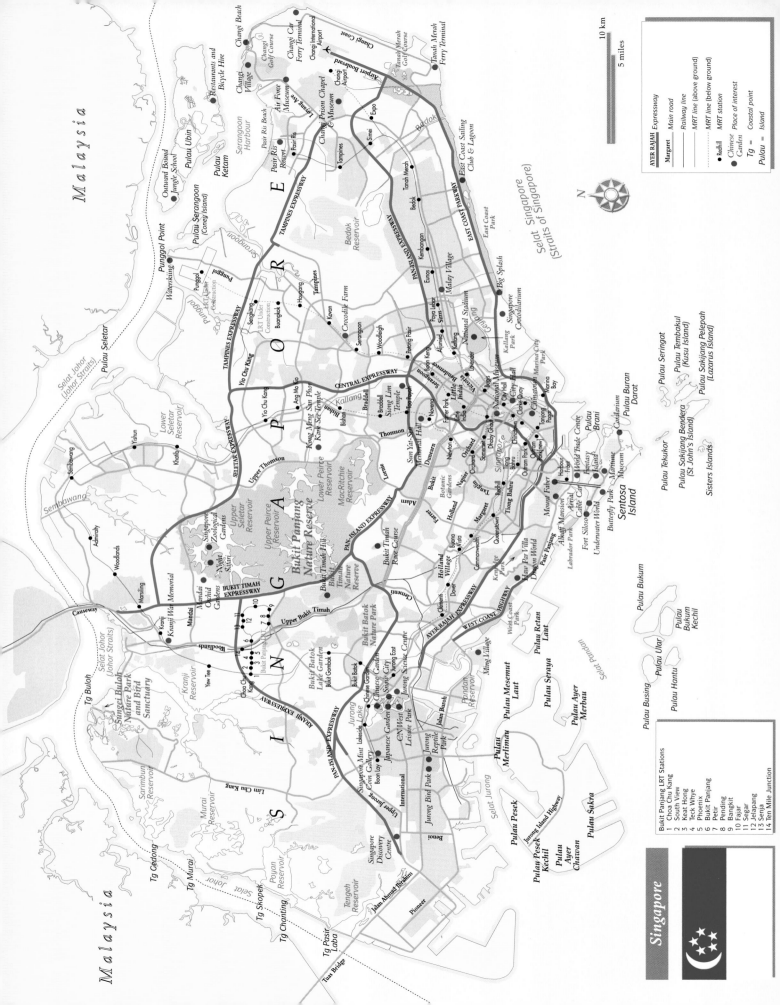